PSYCHE

Unlock Your Subliminal

Mousam Chatterjee

pencil

ISBN 978-93-5559-213-2
© Mousam Chatterjee 2022
Published in India 2022 by Pencil

A brand of
One Point Six Technologies Pvt. Ltd.
123, Building J2, Shram Seva Premises,
Wadala Truck Terminal, Wadala (E)
Mumbai 400037, Maharashtra, INDIA
E connect@thepencilapp.com
W www.thepencilapp.com

Author biography

Mousam Chatterjee is the author behind @Formula Awesome. He is an Animator, designer, editor, artist, director, and aspiring actor/model. His work across multiple disciplines broadly addresses narratives of human experience. As an animator, Jonathan has had established his own international studio named 'animation door' which is still running successfully worldwide. As an artist and illustrator, he has had his art exhibited on Instagram. He also learned as an MMA Fighter and started his career in the acting industry., he graduated from a well-known film school, Whistling Woods International in Mumbai, India.

CONTENTS

Acknowledgements

The book you're gasping right now contains probably the most impressive lessons accessible to you on our planet today. It is special in the entirety of the distribution—you'll be lucky to take advantage of the thinking about the people who are forever associated with the most powerful Source of Energy '*Our Mind*'. My previously thought is that assuming you're not yet prepared to peruse and apply this extraordinary insight, then, at that point, I encourage you to just convey this book with you for half a month. Permit the energy that it contains to saturate through any opposition that your body/brain may offer, and allow it to resound with that inward spot that is undefined and boundaryless—this is the thing that is regularly called your spirit. This is a vast expanse of vibration.

As Einstein once noticed, "*Nothing occurs until something moves*"— that is, everything vibrates to a specific quantifiable recurrence. To sum up, a perception I've presented for a long time now: "*When you change how you check out things, the things you see change.*" You're going to see and experience an entirely different world-changing just before your eyes. This is the world made by a Source of Energy that needs you to reconnect to it and carry on with an existence of happy prosperity. Much obliged to you, <u>I love you—ALL OF YOU.</u>—**Mousam**

Also,

This book has been composed for data purposes as it were. Every effort has been made to make this book as completely accurate as could be expected. Nonetheless, there might be botches in typography or content. Additionally, this book gives data just up to the distributing date. Consequently, this digital book ought to be utilized as a guide - not as a definitive source. The motivation behind this digital book is to instruct. The creator and the distributor try not to warrant that the data contained in this book is completely complete and will not be liable for any blunders or oversights. The creator and distributor will have neither risk nor obligation to any individual or substance concerning any misfortune or harm caused or claimed to be caused straightforwardly or in a roundabout way by this digital book.

Introduction

A ton has been expounded on the idea of the psyche and creating mental strength for better progress. We as a whole know a ton of the writing concerning the law of fascination, dominating the psyche, and growing positive routines to endure forever. However, truly fostering these rehearses reliably over the long haul is very troublesome. It is particularly troublesome when confronted with advanced difficulties which appear to be intended to deplete away our energy. Such depletes can incorporate web-based media, WiFi, bills, and costs, broken connections, natural poisons, cell phones, liquor, sugar, caffeine, the rundown continues.

Fostering a solid outlook involves predictable practice over delayed timeframes. It requires a feeling of reasonableness and discipline that is very frequently neglected. It would be a misstep to believe that the law of fascination is simple or that reflection will promptly reduce misery. Yet, assuming you truly focus on fostering your mentality so that you can zero in on what you need over the long haul, then, at that point, the results will be extraordinary. To do as such, you should figure out how to depend on yourself. According to Indian philosopher Krishnamurti -

"*A hypothesis dependent on one more man's involvement with issues of the mind or an internal life has no importance by any means…. We need to release it totally because we need to remain solitary.*"

Part 1

Understanding the Mind

The initial phase in understanding the brain is to understand that your contemplations are what decide your ordinary encounters. This is the essential reason for every profound message and elusive way of thinking. It is additionally reflected in numerous logical circles like quantum mechanics. Individuals have specific idea designs that they got from the more extensive society, from their folks, from gatherings and associations and so forth they then, at that point, project these idea designs onto their environmental factors. Furthermore they then, at that point, erroneously trust that their projections and translations are 'reality'. Be that as it may, the fact of the matter is diverse for everyone, contingent upon their specific musings. This is the reason there is such a lot of variety on the planet today.

Thoughts Become Things

A center part of spiritual development lies in eliminating all of the thought designs that we have gotten when we were youthful. These were simply modified into us. At the point when we figure out how to eliminate and reinstall various thoughts and beliefs is the point at which we begin to come into our actual independence as bosses over our psyches.

Furthermore, this is somewhat why meditation is suggested across times and societies. We can smoothly notice our musings designs without response or contribution. This is one of the main ways that we can see things dispassionately. In any case, we will quite often relate to our sexual orientation, political philosophies, ethnicity, or class. Furthermore, we normally see this as 'right' because of our restricted educational experience.

Individuals who don't comprehend the force of their personalities are generally lost as they can't recognize as cognizant makers of their reality. They will reliably see a major problem with the world and inquire as to why it is so hard to fight with. Understanding the power of thoughts is the initial step to individual authority.

The Insanity of the Mind

According to the viewpoint of spiritual frameworks, the psyche is unreasonable, silly, and crazy. We are needed to notice the psyche and disengage from it to see its brokenness. Yet, we can likewise notice this brokenness on a more excellent scale with the conflicts, disdain, natural obliteration, bigotry, sexism, homophobia, political assaults, broken connections, government spying programs, cell phone addictions, medical conditions, and that's just the beginning. Something is somewhat broken with the human people, and this is a consequence of a huge number of psyches that are not perfectly located.

Online media and incorporated media likewise serve to program these personalities into a condition of debilitation and dread. Furthermore publicizing additionally has a significant disastrous exertion as it urges individuals to smoke cigarettes, drink liquor, and devour sugar and caffeine. A significant highlight recall is that you are not insusceptible to promoting regardless of whether you think you are. At the point when you see something, it has a psychological effect on your inner mind. So except if you switch off your television and try not to go into a shop, you are a survivor of promoting.

Logical Discoveries and Psychological Observations

There are some logical disclosures and mental perceptions which may be of interest in seeing how the psyche functions.

These include:

1. The psyche can't recognize genuine and fanciful.

2. 95% of your movement is subliminal (take a stab at being deliberately mindful of each key you type on your PC. Your advancement will be inconceivably decreased.)

3. Your psyche has put away all that has at any point occurred as far as you might be concerned, similar to a monstrous PC

4. We are besieged with 2 million pieces of information consistently. It is the occupation of the subliminal to channel through all of this.

5. The cognizant psyche recalls between 5-9 bits of data. This data is passed to the subliminal for handling to let loose cognizant space.

6. The vast majority of our energy consumption goes towards the mind.

These revelations have significant ramifications. If most of our lives are satisfied by the psyche, it follows that we should attempt to control our psyche mind rather than our cognizant capacities. As per Carl Jung - "*Until you make the oblivious cognizant, it will coordinate your life and you will call it destiny*". Programming of the subliminal for cognizant development is the premise of certifications that's more self-spellbinding for strengthening. Be that as it may, alongside these procedures, there are different interesting points to make a positive attitude for development and satisfaction.

Part 2

The Most Effective Method To Develop Mental Strength

Understanding that your considerations decide your current circumstance and that you can order your considerations is the initial step. However, focusing on an everyday schedule of creating mental and enthusiastic strength is something totally different. It takes discipline, character, and persistence. The possibility that we can simply show what we need is a bit misinformed. The truth of the matter is that you might have spent the last 30 or 40a long times against showing.

Focusing in on stress and stress, eating some unacceptable food sources, in harmful connections, with restricting convictions that have been with you since adolescence. These are not eliminated for the time being. It can require a very long time to free yourself of specific considerations and thoughts, and you must be continually watchful with regards to what you are thinking and what you are burning through.

Explore Different Avenues Regarding Exercise

Thankfully, there are many ways to increase your mental and emotional power. And it has never been easier to embark on a campaign of self-development than it is today with all of the resources at your disposal, especially with the internet and instant communications. We have all of the tools. We just need some willpower and determination.

One fundamental method for developing mental fortitude is with an activity schedule. Work out your objectives and goals and check whether you can stay with them. This may seem like extremely essential and major guidance. Be that as it may, both eating regimens also practice give important bits of knowledge into our conduct, and they are the two essential modalities that psychological strength can be based upon. On the off chance that you don't monitor the essentials, you will run into hardships later on. Attempting to turn into an expert of the psyche while gazing at a TV the entire day and eating frozen yogurt is definitely not practical. Diet and exercise can be utilized to fabricate a solid person and a sound body also mind.

Explore Different Avenues Regarding Diet

Diet is somewhere else to begin creating mental strength. I think we as a whole comprehend that we will work better without caffeine, sugar, frozen yogurt, also other handled items. However many individuals can't go a single week without those things which upset mental prosperity. Attempt and check whether you can go on a specific eating routine for seven days. Furthermore when you try not to adhere to it, attempt and analyze why this is the situation. You will start to acknowledge what meant for you are by the climate, how being in a shop or entering a café made you act naturally and purchase a thing that you knew was undesirable. All in all, you have not really settled your conduct.

The Importance of the Surrounding Environment

For mental strength, attempt to control the climate first. In thisway, you will be making a move to fall flat. Controlling theclimate for mental strength will imply that you utilize theidea of moderation however much as could be expected. The less data andinterruptions you have as a rule, the more clear the psyche will be. So perfectyour room and your office, even the documents on your pc. This will have apositive effect on your psychological prosperity. Individuals who will more often than not crowdthings observe new mental energy when they let go of their numerousassets and send them to the waste store. Limit the time you spendon TV and switch off your telephone around evening time. Disposing of link isadditionally really smart.

Indeed, even things like making your bed in the first part of the day and investing some energyout in nature can truly assist with setting the brain up. One more method ofdepicting the idea of the universe being a result of psyche is that'the external mirrors the inward'. We can undoubtedly tell the character of anindividual by the condition of their room. It tends to be fanaticallyslick and clean or it very well may be similar as a dump. Preferably, it very well may be slick andefficient with a couple of things tossed around to a great extent. Understandingthe significance of the climate is a significant disclosure. It impliesthat we can change outer items and circumstances that will emphaticallyponder our inner state, as well as the other way around.

Promoting and Media - The Negative Mental Devices

The damaging idea of promoting and the media turns out to be more significant when individuals begin to peer inside and comprehend the power of their considerations. Assuming most of our activities are subliminal and publicizing and media are explicitly focused on controlling our current circumstance, then, at that point, they have an enormous say in the way we act. Logical information has shown that individuals are survivors of publicizing any event when they view themselves as impenetrable.

At the point when we see something, our cognizant personalities probably won't take it in. Your psyche does.

So nearly as a matter of course, we are on the whole casualties of the general climate which is pointed toward undermining our activities. What's more, it works effectively, considering that industrialism is spinning out of control and individuals are presently paying almost $1,000 for telephones alone while ethics and morals fall by the wayside. Assuming you are not kidding about fostering your psyche, then, at that point, it needs to be pretty much as clear as could be expected. Diminish your openness to publicizing and media where proper. Media is to a great extent negative. Furthermore, your subliminal psyche is going to ingest negative material which will be reflected in your cognizant day-by-day exercises. It is rarely a decent thought to effectively search out this negative data.

The vast majority fool themselves into accepting that they need to"stay in contact with the real world", which is entertaining to individuals who see how reality works. Try not to let futile data frompublicizing, the media, or others occupy significant intellectual room naturally. To restrict this openness, you want to get somewhat coordinated and establish an engaging climate that is helpful for consistent discernment.

Part 3

Best Practices for Serious Mental Development

When you have a decent climate with a sensible eating routine and standard workout, you can research rehearses that are all the more straightforwardly orientated towards the mental turn of events. Recall that everything that you do is extending the brain to a certain extent, regardless of whether it is diet, exercise, composing, or strolling. However, we want to utilize the most immediate strategies, and we likewise need to keep away from designs that don't extend the psyche. Coming up next are the accepted procedures for you to truly ace your very own brain research. To continue quickly, then, at that point, attempt one or some of these models. How frequently and at what force you need to do these practices is dependent upon you.

#1 - Meditation

Meditation should not shock anybody as the most ideal sort of practice for the mental turn of events. It includes sitting discreetly(in a perfect world in a lotus position) and noticing the developments of the brain. Later a timeframe, the psyche begins to quieten down and turn less unglued. You will turn out to be less responsive to outside occasions and be capable to screen and control your considerations all the more proficiently. The two most famous sorts of meditation are Vipassana and supernatural Meditation. Both of these have a broad assemblage of logical writing relating to their advantages. There is not any justification for not impelling a normal meditation schedule. It is confirmed by science, rehearsed by some significant level people, and has noteworthy roots in otherworldly frameworks. Double a day for 20 minutes is the suggested period for ideal results, morning and evening. You can likewise think about an extraordinary course for seven days to truly get everything rolling.

#2 - Yoga

Yoga is an act of body development including the breath, fixation, equilibrium, adaptability, and actual strength. When the developments are executed in a specific manner the expert comes into a stream state and can finish the entire extended daily practice easily. The coordination of fixation, breathing, and physical effort are ideal for quelling the psyche. It is preposterous to expect to practice the daily schedule while the brain is dynamic, as it gets in the way. Yoga is best finished when it turns into a customary propensity that doesn't need a cognizant idea.

#3 - Fasting

However this may be portrayed as an outrageous strategy, fasting is one of the most ideal ways to dominate your brain. Food is more vital to a person than whatever else. Surrendering nourishment for a huge time of time can have many advantages and takes staggering resolve. Moreover, fasting is the main thing that has been demonstrated to expand life span in rodents and people perform best when they are somewhat ravenous. There are various sorts of quick, for example, water quick, a dry quick, a juice quick, and so on Considering a 3-day squeeze quick once per month for a passionate and mental detox.

#4 - Mindfulness

Mindfulness takes many structures and there is a wide assortment of mindfulness rehearses. It truly includes staying alert at customary stretches for the day. Mindfulness can be joined with a reflection for ga greatest outcomes. In reflection, we are profoundly "non-centered" for 20 minutes or so double a day. With mindfulness, we are essentially more mindful of things at periods all through our working day. For instance, we may leave our work areas like clockwork and just be aware of our relax briefly to segregate us from our errands. Mindfulness is regularly connected with the breath, as this is a speedy course to the current second.

#5 - Concentration

There are numerous different procedures to expand concentration. You could zero in on a candle fire for five minutes per day. You can likewise zero in on the highest point of your nose or your breath. Most profound professionals suggest no longer than 10 minutes of extreme concentration on anything. Unintentionally, ten minutes is the most extreme measure of time that an individual can strongly zero in on anything, as per the logical examination. There is a wide assortment of concentration procedures that you can utilize.

#6 - Any Practice with Passion or Intensity

Assuming you can find something that you are truly energetic with regards to then, at that point, you can keep on zeroing in on this with resolute power. This can incorporate canvas, singing, moving, combative techniques, making a business, or anything that you truly give 100% of your psychological consideration towards. This is because you will not have the opportunity to empower negative musings or feelings as every one of your assets is pointed towards one specific action. This is perhaps the best way to control the psyche and eliminate damaging inclinations. Yet, except if you are truly enthusiastic with regards to something, it tends to be hard to create the fixation and resolution to own it. To this end, the vast majority abandon their goals later in the underlying stage.

Progressed Protocols

There are a few techniques you can utilize to acquirecommand over the brain. They are planned with the goal that you will makeforward leaps that will remain to you over the long haul. Consider an11-day quiet retreat in a tranquil area, out in nature. During thisquiet retreat, you will ponder double a day, complete a yoga schedule,what's more adhere to a vegetarian diet without liquor, sugar, or handled food sources.You ought to likewise be totally taken out from innovation during this time.

You will help such a system monstrously for various reasons. Youcan notice the difference from the quiet retreat and the craziness andclamor of the regular climate. You can likewise notice the differenceat the point when you once again introduce specific food sources once more into your eating routine. You should pointfor some sort of seclusive practice to reconnect like clockwork or something like that.It will assist you with understanding that the ordinary workplace iscrazy and there you can accomplish a quiet condition of being without awild brain producing trepidation and nervousness constantly.

Part 4

The Subconscious Mind and Self-Programming Strategies

A decent analogy is that the human brain resembles a PC program. It takes in input from an assortment of sources and produces yield. Yet we are not mindful of all that we are taking in subliminally. The vast majority of our action is administered by the subliminal gone against the cognizant psyche. As per Earl Nightingale -"*Whatever we plant in our psyche mind and support with redundancy and feeling will one day become a reality*"

Affirmations

Affirmations are a powerful instrument to program ourselves for individual furthermore business achievement. Recollect when certifying to utilize the present tense. "*I'm gifted*" or "*I'm rich*" is better than "*I will be capable*" or "*I will be rich*". One more highlight kept in mind is that affirmations work best when the brain is in an open state. So affirmations ought to be involved the first thing or then again late around evening time. Some other chance to rehash your affirmations is during contemplation when they can truly soak in without opposition.

Affirmations work however they must be rehashed over and over so truly so our psyche can truly receive the message clearly and clear. For most extreme outcomes, they should be expressed (inside or without holding back) during contemplation or in the waking or evening hours. It ought to likewise be born as a main priority that certain individuals have unquestionably profound feelings concerning adore, cash, or sexuality. At a principal level, an individual may not accept that they are contemptible of adoration or fondness. On such occasions, affirmations may not work and diet, self-assessment, yoga also contemplation may be generally expected to truly stir up the individual's mentality into a positive state.

There have been situations where advisors entranced patients into a positive conviction (with their assent). Inevitably, the basic negative conviction reappeared. This proposes that the conviction is either very much established or that it comes from someplace further than the subliminal psyche. Regardless, join affirmations with a reflection for best outcomes, as they take care of business generally. Assuming that you can make your affirmations into a sonnet that rhymes then your inner mind will rehash it reliably, similar to how a melody stalls out in your head. This is everything method you can manage to assume you have distinguished a restricting conviction and need to dispose of it. Where conceivable, attempt to feel the attestation as a positive feeling. This will supercharge it with energy what's more assist it with showing.

You should step through a web-based examination to see where you have restricting convictions. They might associate with confidence, connections, cash, wealth, or then again a joy. In this example, you can attempt to make a few affirmations utilizing various terms and tenses to explore this tacky conviction all the more quickly. For instance:

- *"I am rich"*

- *"I have always been rich"*

- "Riches are waiting for me"

- "I love being so financially abundant"

- "People see me as very affluent"

- "I have so many sources of income"

- "I always have enough money"

- "Money is a mental abstraction and I can just think more of it"

- "Because money is so common it is easy to collect some"

- "I love thinking about and making money"

- "Money was always easy for me to attract"

- "Poverty and abundance are just states of mind"

With affirmations, it is better overall to utilize the current state and to try not to invalidate proclamations, for example, "*I'm not in destitution*". Very much like the cerebrum can't recognize genuine and fanciful, it additionally does not get the reputation. All it hears is "neediness".

Self Programming Strategies

There are different techniques you can use to program your brain. Recall that the time you are simply waking and the time that you are settling down to rest are the best occasions for self-programming. Reflection is another key time.

Be that as it may, you need to use the remainder of the day however much as could be expected to put yourself into a positive perspective. On the off chance that you have a work area work, then, at that point, you are stuck on a PC for 8 hours per day. You should capitalize on it. Pay attention to old-style music for several hours a day. Binaural beats and theta brainwave entrainment tracks are accessible on Youtube and different destinations.

Then again, record yourself saying enabling affirmations and tune into it for 60 minutes. Subliminally, the assertions *"I'm rich"*, *"I'm appealing"*, *"I'm canny"* will soak in and begin to show in your daily existence.

You could likewise consider clear dreaming or considering an advisor to be a method for getting to the psyche. There are an enormous number of self-programming techniques accessible. Simply pick a couple and stick with them for a reliable timeframe.

Keep in mind, self-programming comprises two sections. The first is the thing that you program yourself with. The second is the thing that you can hide out. You may be letting yourself know how appealing you are, yet all at once other individuals and the world may jump at the chance to tell you in any case. Make a clean work and individual climate and dispose of individuals who channel your energy. Additionally, limit time invested via online media and energy spent uncovered to promotions, all things considered.

The Subconscious Mind

Our psyche manages our conduct. This is a logical reality just as a peculiarity reported by analysts Carl Jung and Sigmund Freud. It has likewise been referenced in antiquated texts like the Vedasfurthermore by otherworldly researchers all through the ages. We want to make systems to reconstruct our subliminal in manners that are more helpful to our prosperity. Our psyche minds have gotten different inclinations from birth that are still with us today. We are moreover enduring an onslaught (in a real sense) with promoting that besieges our faculties almost all day, every day. This incorporates on the web, where we are burning through a large portion of our lives, just as in the actual climate, where we see boards furthermore things available to be purchased in shops. We should be extremely cautious with regards to what we ingest intellectually, truly, and inwardly. Probably the most ideal way to reinvent our psyche is by utilizing affirmations.

Part 5

Law of Attraction v Shadow Work

There are two significant surges of thought inside the brain science andotherworldly areas. Individuals who observe the law of fascination trust thatwhat you thoroughly consider builds up speed time and draws in additionalpositive considerations. Assuming we can tune our vibration towards things thatfulfill us, then, at that point, this energy will increment and being glad willbecome easier and simpler.

However, there are other people who suggest a similarly compelling case. Eachindividual has a shadow side that is curbed by present day culture, if thisshadow side isn't examined and permitted to communicate itself thoughts, then, at that point, it willkeep on hiding in our inner mind, attacking our satisfaction. Whatever is inside us should be handledwhat's more communicated somehow or another. It is a regularly acknowledged logicalrule that energy can't be made or annihilated, however it tends to bechanged.

A Deeper Look Into the Shadow

Shadow brain science was first promoted by the impending professorial Jung. The shadow is simply the oblivious perspective that we can not deliberately relate to. There are certain angles of the shadow side.

"*People Pleasers*" need to begin relating to their resentment and start telling individuals to get lost. But since they were brought up to regard others and be "*great*", they find it hard to intentionally comprehend that denying individuals can be immensely natural, fulfilling, and normal. All things considered, they take on more work than they ought to and end up pushed, accepting that sabotaging their mental and enthusiastic prosperity is some way or another a 'positive' thing.

Generally, notwithstanding, the shadow displays negative propensities. It contains deep fears and weaknesses. It then, at that point, projects these apprehensions and securities onto others. Frequently, individuals will extend their negative tendencies onto others to manage their aggravation. It is the following best thing to have the option to face it inside themselves, which is undeniably more troublesome.

For Jung, the most ideal way to investigate the Shadow side was through dreamwork and emblematic investigation. The Shadow was alluded to as the "*Oblivious*" underway of both Sigmund Freud and Friedrich Nietzsche. The idea of ShadowSelf has become substantially more famous as of late due to the earlier strength of the law of fascination. More individuals than any time in recent memory are involved in dreamwork and self-evaluation polls to break up shadow inclinations and carry the shadow self to the bleeding edge of the cognizant mind.

The Law of Attraction

The Law of Attraction was first advocated by Jerry and Esther Hickson in the 2006 film "*The Secret*". They expressed to channel a non-physical substance known as Abraham. Jerry Hicks died from a malignant growth in 2011, driving numerous to scrutinize the validness of the development.

However, Esther Hicks is still a lot of dynamics and has a monstrous after. Moreover, the Law of Attraction is exhibited or suggested in numerous authentic social orders and profound texts. It isn't the sole space of the Hicks, however, they are the ones who have carried it to the public mindfulness in a 21st-century setting.

The Law of Attraction appears to be legit and does more to clarify why certain individuals are fruitful and others are not more than anything else. Be that as it may, the total arrangement of lessons adds a great deal more and dive into complex circumstances that reach out a long way past zeroing in on certain contemplations. Furthermore, it puts another accentuation on wants and feelings.

These were seen as *'grimy'* from an Eastern otherworldly viewpoint, where we acquire quite a bit of our elusive data from. Such mutilations have, however, persuaded individuals that cravings and feelings are some way or another wickedness, nothing could be further from reality. In addition, a lot of accentuation has been put on mental considerations, when it is the passionate vibrations that are what gives solidarity to the appearance. The law of fascination depends on sentiments rather than considerations, which is a new worldview.

Which One Should I Do

Fortunately, there is no requirement for segregation. Shadow work furthermore a positive mentality can both effectively be applied together. There is no need to agree with one gathering '*against*' the other. This is both trivial furthermore counterproductive. All things considered, embrace the smartest possible solution. You might observe that accomplishing energy stir raises stowed away shadows and that zeroing in on understanding the Shadow attempts to build your levels of energy.

A decent trade-off could be to accomplish both shadow work and keep a positive brain science, yet attempt to zero in erring on positive brain science. It additionally assists with seeing that there is a distinction between overlooking something and zeroing in on the positive side of things. To meet your challenges head-on and face them forthrightly. Simultaneously, attempt to plan and be hopeful concerning what it has available for you. Try not to keep away from the past and your internal evil presences, as this has been recognized as the main obstacle to future development and advancement. Passionate aversion is likewise the main source of misery as per a few specialists in the area of brain science. It can be an extreme line to adjust between the two. However, to create a truly solid outlook, you need to zero in on both.

Part 6

Creativity and Imagination as Tools for Development

The sheer force of the creative mind has not been given its due in by the same token religion, science, or otherworldliness. These look to give the understudy arrangement of the method of activity as to how to live and act. However, innovativeness and creative mind are without equal and are interestingly individual practices. There is no framework or design for creative minds or innovative work.

How Does the Imagination Work

It very well may be somewhat hard to depict precisely what a creative mind is and how it functions. Yet, it bears a likeness to reflection as far as dissolving issues and tracking down arrangements Since when utilizing the creative mind, the individual is in a modified condition of cognizance. There is no real way to make a magnificent verse or an amazing artwork at the point when the legitimate side of the cerebrum is actuated. Since the coherent side of the cerebrum needs to comprehend the reason why each piece is set in a certain way and needs to work consecutively in an ABC style. This isn't the ticket innovativeness works, which examinations and perceives how things work out without focusing on standard levelheadedness.

It is the creative mind, not intelligent cycles, that is liable for most human accomplishments. Steve Jobs utilized his creative mind to make an altogether new item range that had never been seen. Tesla is doing likewise with his Space X and electric vehicle projects. These are new standards. Also, think about that the best and generally remarkable prodigies might not have even gone to class. As indicated by Edward Bachlater he completed his studies - "*it will take me five years to fail to remember all I have been educated*". Einstein has no confidence in school and broadly expressed that

"Rationale will get you from A to B. Creative mind will go anyplace".

The creative mind is an incredibly integral asset when you convey it accurately and it can produce an enormous number of recuperating benefits. This is one more contention for the Law of Attraction advocates. Sensibly, you might see that you have an annoying issue that you want to investigate.

In any case, on the off chance that you are exceptionally inventive and divert this in the right heading towards a center enthusiasm, your issues will disintegrate minus any additional examination. Moreover, some innovative defenders declare that the creative mind is a method of carrying the subliminal to the cognizant. Along these lines, you can paint composition or image about an issue that you can't deliberately relate to. You probably won't comprehend the reason why you feel great in the wake of doing a certain piece of innovative work, yet it very well maybe because it addresses inward issues that can't be intentionally examined or talked about. The way that the psyche conveys is in pictures and representations, not in rationale or text. This is the thing that kids frequently do when they play and paint. In any case, broad utilization of innovativeness and the creative mind can do ponders for self-advancement and mental strength.

How Do I Use My Imagination

It tends to be difficult to make a framework or construction concerning thecreative mind because by its very nature it doesn't adjust todesigns or anything moving toward objective standards. The best thingthat you can do is to truly concede to an imaginative cycle and watch the enchantment unfurl. Perhaps the best methodology is to:

(a) Create 100 compositions in a month.

(b) Write 1000 imaginative words every day for a month.

(c) Try to envision yourself in an ideal setting at power for10 minutes every day

Be that as it may, it is incredibly hard to get individuals to do thesebasic assignments. This is on the grounds that individuals consistently need to know "why" andarrive at a sane objective. Yet, these cycles will stir up your psyche andopen up your innovative awareness. You will acquire bits of knowledge from yourartworks or works en route.

Indeed, you will improve resultsassuming you don't have an objective as a primary concern with these works/artistic creations/perceptions, like a financial prize. Assuming you can accomplish somethinglike this the advantages will be tremendous. As an extra suggestion, youtry not to need to figure out how to paint in any capacity or even how to compose orimagine the 'right' way. These are your inventive works. Simply dothem and receive the rewards of your own imagination.

Innovative Wealth Manifestation Tricks

There are some innovative techniques that you can send to stunt your cerebrum into a plenitude outlook. In numerous ways, you can deal with it like a game. The mind is accustomed to creating stress and dread at all occasions corresponding to cash. You want to attempt to get around this instilled propensity by claiming to be affluent. The cerebrum can't recognize genuine and nonexistent peculiarities, as shown by ongoing logical investigations. Think about what happens when you ponder your cherished food - your body begins reacting organically. Your stomach will begin to protest and you may even begin salivating, regardless of no actual food being available. The more you ponder food, the 'hungrier' your body becomes. Moreover, the universe doesn't separate between genuine and nonexistent, so you can utilize inventive practices to fool yourself into considering consideration abundance.

• **Trick One**- Carry cash consistently. Where conceivable, ensure that your wallet is brimming with cash. It is smarter to have it on you. Along these lines, make sure to tip 20% consistently. Both of these procedures have two critical impacts. The first is that you will get into the mentality of somebody rich, as you will be utilized to continually having sufficient money and continually tipping well. The second is that others view you as affluent furthermore begin appearing for you. They are likewise used to seeing you having cash and being rich and partnering your persona with abundance.

• **Trick Two**- Hang out with the Rich. Rich individuals (i.e a bounty mentality) are accustomed to having abundance consistently. They try not to ponder neediness or bills by any means. Assuming you can offshoot yourself with these individuals then their energy and convictions will rub off on you. To turn into the best legal advisor in your space, then, at that point, you want to arrange and connect yourself with these individuals. Not for the 'information', but rather to attempt to copy their attitude that draws in legitimate mastery.

• **Trick Three**- Be thankful. Appreciation is the sacred goal of appearance. It enjoys an upper hand over appearance since it can fulfill you, while appearances will quite often be brief. Assuming you can dominate both appearance and appreciation, then, at that point, you are an expert. Since you will show what you need furthermore currently keen on what you have. Moreover, when you are appreciative for what you have effectively shown, the universe demonstrates you more things to be thankful for and indication becomes simpler.

Part 7

Immersion in Different Fields

Drenching is seemingly one of the speediest and most ideal ways to improve your psychological and enthusiastic molding. It is additionally one of the hardest. Suppose you went through a year learning Mandarin Chinese while all the while learning C programming and Brazilian Ju-Jitsu. It would be a gigantically troublesome year for you. It would likewise be one of the generally fulfilling assuming that you had the option to pull it off.

This is because every one of these spaces will show your cerebrum unique things. At the point when individuals learn things in a homeroom learning it is as a rule the most noticeably terrible kind - repetition taking in perusing from a screen. This is not a solid method for learning things and is additionally extremely dreary.

The way that individuals learn is just as significant as the subject matter. So learning a language while conversing with individuals is in no way like taking in language from a book. What's more, attempting to make another program in a programming language is unique about learning it in a study hall. Learning each of the three of these is simply not sensible in the advanced climate. However, you could consider doing one of them, in some measure low maintenance. Furthermore, there are additionally various types of inundation.

Immersion Strategies

We have as of now referenced two of the best submersion systems accessible. These are escalated painting and concentrated composition. Both of these draw on your imaginative resources so you can make them more grounded. Inventiveness is a fantastic instrument that you can use in almost any specific situation. When you open up your innovativeness only a tad, you can gather speed what's more make development and the creative mind as central parts of your presence. Yet, it generally takes responsibility and self-discipline toward the beginning to inundate yourself in the innovative flow. Think about that MarkZuckerberg openly posted that how planned to go through a year learning Mandarin Chinese. Shrewd individuals are continually searching for approaches to grow their psychological abilities.

Travel is quite possibly the most well-known submersion strategy accessible. Figuring out how various individuals think and act is superb for contrast against your very own qualities and convictions. The starkest illustration of this is when individuals of the West go to places like India and Thailand in the East. While individuals in the West are objective orientated and live in the future, individuals of the East will quite often live at the time more (this has its arrangement of downsides, as they for the most part don't appear to be persuaded enough as far as self-improvement).

Many individuals go through something like an extended time of their lives voyaging. Be that as it may, they will generally go above and beyond about it. They frequently do it close to the furthest limit of their lives and attempt to fit in whatever number spots as would be prudent like checking boxes off an agenda. When voyaging, it is ideal to invest longer energy periods in a set area to truly soak up the way of life.

You can inundate yourself with anything. Attempt to drench yourself in moderation for a month. No television, cell phone, no undesirable food, web-based media, no PC, a perfect work area, a spotless room, a little arrangement of garments, and so forth Recall that 21 days is the time it takes to use a propensity. So assuming you figure out how to finish with something for more than 21 days, then, at that point, you can convey this propensity forward with undeniably less exertion than when you began.

Painful Immersion Practice - The Best Kind

One of the most helpful methods that you can figure out how to create a solid mental structure is to observe what you disdain and do it seriously on the other hand attempt to do something contrary to what you are ordinarily used to doing. In the advanced world, individuals are determined to attempt to be agreeable. The greatest apprehension about somebody in the advanced time is to lose their pay so they couldn't manage the cost of satellite TV or a cell phone charge, both of which don't contribute any genuine worthwhile eating valuable intellectual space.

An old Stoic practice is to work on being pretty much as poor as feasible for a set measure of time. This may sound weird. Be that as it may, there is entirely all to fear. It is cutting edge comforts that are a reason for much pain, just as the steady making progress toward more and to an ever-increasing extent. At the point when you stand up to your feelings of trepidation so straightforwardly, they lose a parcel of their energy. They are just so strong when you don't take a gander at them. This could likewise be known as a structure of shadow work as straightforwardly defying fears.

You can without much of a stretch find your feelings of dread through some experimental writing and ask yourself a few inquiries. Or then again work out a rundown of things that you could never consider doing and wonder why. Assuming that you disdain public talking, take a stab at doing it seriously for a month or something like that. However difficult as it very well might be, you would gain enormous headway.

Be Prepared

Comprehend that submersion won't be a lovely cycle, by what's more huge. However, it will be exceptionally remunerating eventually. Would you be able to recall how hard it was the point at which you previously needed to gain proficiency with the letter set and string words together? This is the thing that it seems like when you are learning something unique. This is fundamentally what drenching is. The more unfamiliar the subject (like Mandarin Chinese or military craftsmanship)the more prominent the advantages. It will extend your brain in manners that it is not used to being extended.

It is additionally worth thinking about that the huge measure of undertakings is deserted right off the bat. The vast majority finish their yearly goals two weeks into January. Before leaving on a venture that could take you90 days, be certain that you are ready and that you are totally100% sure that you need to do it.

Part 8

Getting Alternative Structures

Perhaps the most ideal way to extend the psyche is to peruse and investigate from a wide range of fields of study. In the West, we are sure that the logical strategy is awesome and the one in particular that works. However we can't disregard the way that our nations are wiped out, the planet contaminated, and individuals are generally dependent on innovation. Self-destruction rates are out of this world and individuals are catching various sicknesses that were not there previously.

Our perspective and comprehension are restricted not exclusively to our geological area yet additionally to our time. On the off chance that Western science was to blend in with Traditional Chinese Medicine and Ayurveda rather than excusing these two frameworks, then, at that point, more headway would be made. In any case, it tends to be useful to see and comprehend various structures to reinforce our personalities. Nonetheless, be careful about perusing as well as much data and turning it into something like a theoretical scholar with next to no true applications. According to Seneca the Stoic -

"Be careful, however, lest this reading of many authors and books of every sort may tend to make you discursive and unsteady. You must linger among a limited number of master thinkers, and digest their works if you would derive ideas which shall win firm hold in your mind."

Attempt to snag a few distinct ways of thinking and perspectives to all the more likely see how things work rather than indiscriminately excusing them out of the container. Here are some other options structures or methods of reasoning that you can take on. Take them one at a time.

Astrology

The essential sort of astrology comes from Indian sacred writings known asthe Vedas. Be that as it may, astrology has its underlying foundations in every single antiquated culturefor example, the Native Americans and Shamanic societies. Astrology isknown as the respectable science among mystics and the procedure isgiven incredible conspicuousness, particularly in India. Western and Vedic astrologyare two separate fields that place accentuation on various planetarypositions. The principle motivation behind astrology is that you can find yourpropensities and comprehend your character better for more profoundcontemplation.

Ayurveda

Ayurveda is the sister study of soothsaying and began in

India. Ayurveda portrays three sorts of energy - Vata, Pitta, and Kapha.

Every individual is one of 11 mixes of these components and give

this mix proposals are given concerning exercise,

diet, and contemplation. Ayurveda is ideally suited for clarifying the holes in

sustenance information that Western science tumbles down on.

Hinduism

Hinduism is exceptional among the religions since it isn't as organized or organized rather than its counterparts. There are hundreds of Gods to be revered and Hindus get to choose a God which confers specific advantages. Along these lines, Hinduism is more open and inventive than customary religions which will generally be a little dogmatic and force a conviction framework on you instead of letting you choose.

Presentism

Presentism is the possibility that main the current exists and that the past also what's to come are deceptive. This is because time is only a deception. The inverse of presentism is known as eternalism, where all minutes in time are similarly genuine. Presentism has its underlying foundations in Buddhism, while current logical hypotheses will in general help eternalism to a degree. It has as of late been modernized with the book "The Power of Now" by Eckhart Tolle.

Stoicism

Stoicism is an amazing way of thinking that is about common sense,however it will in general stigmatize feelings as silly. It was established inAthens and was drilled by Marcus Aurelius and Seneca. Other prominentstoics incorporate George Washington and Thomas Jefferson just asPrussian King Frederick the Great. Current specialists incorporate NassimTaleb and Tim Ferris. The thought behind stoicism is tied in with molding andimprovement. So assuming you endured an awful encounter it isbasically fuel for additional development. Stoicism is worried about activity andlacks the capacity to deal with unending discussion, something which is required in thepresent day time of data over-burden.

Traditional Chinese Medicine

Traditional Chinese Medicine (TCM) is a Chinese investigation of wellbeing. The Chinese attitude is unique about the East, and for this reason, it very well may be superb for the brain (seeing things from an inverse perspective is great for mental extension). This part of medicine is given the possibility of Yin and Yang behind the central parts

of everything in the universe. A specific organ will have excessive or insufficient Yin or Yang energy, and medicines are given to address

these insufficiencies. In TCM, energy lines are known as Nadis or Meridians interconnect all around the body. Furthermore, every organ is connected with a specific feeling, like sorrow, satisfaction, or bliss. The ideas of Nadis and Meridians are additionally present in Indian expressions, for example, Ayurveda.

Taoism

Taoism is one more Chinese subject that is covered in secret. It started from a text called the Tao Te Ching, which was composed by a character called Lao Tzu. It accentuation something many refer to as "The Way" which doesn't have anything to do with an unbending construction or discipline. There are no rules, simply delicate remedies with regards to how to follow the rhythms of life. Confucianism is another well-known Chinese philosophy, yet it is more obdurate and has many principles and rules for conduct.

Zen

Zen is tied in with failing to remember the self generally. It is based around the act of Zazen reflection and Zen is a branch-off of Mahayana Buddhism. Zen can't be depicted in words as it is guaranteed to be an encounter instead of an idea. So following quite a while of contemplation, the specialist becomes Zen. Without contemplation, it is impossible to profoundly and sole part of the practice.

Conclusion

End

There is a wide assortment of ways of fostering your attitude for more noteworthy achievement both by and by and monetarily. A decent spot to get everything rolling would be diet, exercise, reflection, and confirmations. These are generally direct and powerful to return the brain to normal in an areally substantial way. When you have a strong handle on these, you can think about subversion strategies and inventive approaches to truly grow your mindfulness. Recall that fostering an attitude will turn into a deep-rooted however completely charming experience. You simply need to investigate negative convictions and intense subject matters for some time before you can truly grow.